T0088709

John Rutter

# Geistliche Chorgesänge von John Rutter

## Acht geistliche Chorgesänge in deutscher Übersetzung

---

## Inhalt


Verzeichnis der Orchestrierungen 3

Blick auf den Tag 4
Der Friede Gottes 15
Eine englische Segnung 21
Für die Schönheit in der Welt 28
Gott segne und behüt dich 39
Gott sei stets in mir 46
Öffne mir die Augen 49
Schau auf die Welt 54


OXFORD
UNIVERSITY PRESS

OXFORD
UNIVERSITY PRESS

Great Clarendon Street, Oxford OX2 6DP,
United Kingdom

Oxford University Press is a department of the University of Oxford.
It furthers the University's objective of excellence in research, scholarship,
and education by publishing worldwide. Oxford is a registered trade mark of
Oxford University Press in the UK and in certain other countries

This collection © Oxford University Press 2023

John Rutter has asserted his right under the Copyright, Designs
and Patents Act, 1988, to be identified as the Composer of these Works

First published 2023

Impression: 1

All rights reserved. No part of this publication may be reproduced,
stored in a retrieval system, or transmitted, in any form or by any means,
without the prior permission in writing of Oxford University Press

Permission to perform the works in this anthology in public
(except in the course of divine worship) should normally be obtained from
a local performing right licensing organization, unless the owner or the occupier
of the premises being used already holds a licence from such an organization.
Likewise, permission to make and exploit a recording of these works
should be obtained from a local mechanical copyright licensing organization

Enquiries concerning reproduction outside the scope of the above
should be directed to the Music Rights Department, Oxford University Press, at
music.permissions.uk@oup.com or at the address above

ISBN 978–0–19–356617–0

Music originated on Sibelius
Printed in Great Britain on acid-free paper by
Halstan & Co. Ltd, Amersham, Bucks.

German language consultant: Norbert Meyn

# Verzeichnis der Orchestrierungen

Die meisten Stücke in diesem Band sind auch als Versionen mit Orchester erhältlich. Partituren und Instrumentalstimmen können bei www.oup.com zum Verleih bestellt und wenn angezeigt auch käuflich erworben werden.

*Blick auf den Tag*
2Fl, Ob, 2Cl, Fg, 2Hrn, Hf, Str (*Verleih*)

*Der Friede Gottes*
Str *(Verleih)*

*Eine englische Segnung*
2Fl, Ob, 2Cl, Fg, 2Hrn, Hf, Str (*Verleih*)

*Für die Schönheit in der Welt*
2Fl, Ob, 2Cl, Fg, 2Hrn, Glsp, Hf, Str *(Verleih und Verkauf)*
Fl, Ob, Hf, Org *(Verkauf)*

*Gott segne und behüt dich*
Str *(Verleih und Verkauf)*
Fl, Ob, Hf, Org *(Verkauf)*

*Schau auf die Welt*
2Fl, Ob, 2Cl, Fg, 2Hrn, Glsp, Hf, Str *(Verleih)*
Fl, Ob, Hf, Org *(Verkauf)*

*Komponiert für die britische Krebsforschungsgesellschaft*
*Anlässlich ihres Dankgottesdienstes in der Kathedrale von Ely am 23. September 2007*

# Blick auf den Tag

(Look to the day)

Text und Musik
**JOHN RUTTER**

Dt. Übers.: Tobias Martin

© Collegium Music Publications 2008 und 2023. Exclusively licensed worldwide to Oxford University Press.
Das Fotokopieren von Musiknoten ist GESETZLICH VERBOTEN.

13
Er - de glänzt in vol - ler Blü - ten - pracht, Strah - lend rings in
earth smells sweet and ev - 'ry flower looks bright, Shin - ing in a
mf
più legato
Ped.
sim.
17
frisch - em Tau wenn dein Blick sie streift.
dew - y light as you wan - der by.
A
SOPRAN und ALT
21
mp
Nimm Dir die Zeit und ge - nieß' den Au - gen - blick;
Tak - ing the time to en - joy each mo - ment;
leggiero
sempre
(con Ped. sempre)

25
cresc.
kos - te die Frucht die am Weg rand liegt,
Tast - ing the fruits spread a - long your way,
cresc.
29
poco f
mf
nimm Dir die Zeit da - für, träum Dei - nen Traum und sprich:
Know - ing there's time to spare, Dreams you can dream and share:
f dolce
mf
33
mp
blick auf den Tag, blick auf den Tag.
Look to the day, look to the day.
mp
mf

B
TENOR und BASS
37
unis. mp cantabile
2. Blick auf den Tag, wenn die Welt ganz
2. Look to the day when the earth is
B
mp legato
Ped.
sim.
41
neu er - grünt; Früh - lings - gruß nach dem Win - ter -
green a - gain: Pro - mise of spring af - ter win - ter's
45
poco cresc.
mf
- schlaf. Weit tönt das Le - ben, wel - ches
sleep. The sounds of life re - turn - ing
cresc.
mf

49
mp
neu er - wacht E - wi - ge Mu - sik der Welt schließ sie in dein
fill the air, Mu-sic that's for - ev - er there for your heart to
mp
53
C
p
Herz. Sä - e die Saat aus der mor - gen
keep. Deep in the earth lay the seed of
p
57
Neu - es sprießt, lei - se und stark bis zur Früh - lings -
life re - newed, Qui - et and strong till the time of

61
mp cresc.
mf
- zeit:
spring:
Le - ben in Spross und Blatt,
Life in each bud and shoot,
mp cresc.
mf
65
mp
Le - ben in Blüt' und Frucht.
Life in each flower and fruit,
Blick auf den Tag, wenn al - les
Look to that day when earth shall
mp
69
grünt.
sing.
p legato

73
D
p
mp
S.
A.
3. Blick auf das Licht; es ver-treibt die Fin - ster - nis;
3. Look to the light that will drive out dark - ness;
T.
B.
p
mp
D
mp
77
mf
f
Blick auf die Kraft die die Angst be - zwingt. Die
Look to the hope that will con-quer fear. God's
mf
f
cresc.
mf
81
Hoff - nung stärkt uns bis der Sieg uns winkt,
strength up - hold us till the fight is won,
mf

84
mf
bis wir un - s're Pflicht ge - tan und der Tag uns
Till we see our task is done when the day is
mf
87
E
mp
naht.
here.
Blick auf den Tag,
Look for that day
T. und B.
Mm
Bassen div.
mp
E
p dolce e legato
90
wenn der Schmerz vo - rü - ber ist:
when there shall be no more pain;
Ped.

93
Kum - mer und Seuf - zen nun ver - geh'n.
Sor - row and sigh - ing shall pass a - way.
(mm)
Ped.
97
Bet' für den Tag der kommt,
Pray for the day to come,
mp
trau dem Tag der naht,
Trust that the day will come,
101 mp
blick auf den Tag, blick auf den Tag.
Look to that day, look to the day.
cresc.

105
F
f
4. Herr, Dir sei Dank, daß Du uns das Le - ben schenkst;
4. Lord, we give thanks for the gifts of life and health;
f
F
f
109
pflanz neu - e Saat - cn in un - ser Herz:
Plant a new seed in our hearts, we pray:
113
Hilf uns zu seh'n, O Herr, die - sen Tag,
Help us to see, O Lord, How it could be,

116
mf
O Herr; Blick auf den Tag, blick auf den
O Lord; Look to the day, look to the
mf
mf
119
Tag,
day,
mp
dim.
blick auf den Tag,
look to the day,
mp
122
rallentando al fine
p
blick auf den Tag.
look to the day.
p
rallentando al fine
p
Ped.

*für den Bischof Thomas McMahon und die Menschen in der Diözese Brentwood im Vereinigten Königreich*

# Der Friede Gottes

## (The peace of God)

Aus dem Book of Common Prayer (1662)
nach Philipper 4, 7
Dt. Übers.: Moritz von Freyhold

**JOHN RUTTER**

© Oxford University Press 1991 und 2023. Das Fotokopieren von Musiknoten ist GESETZLICH VERBOTEN.

13
Wis - sen um Got - tes Lieb' und der des Sohns Je - sus Chris -
know - ledge and love of God, and of his Son Je - sus Christ
16
A
p dolce
S.
A.
- tus:
our Lord:
Der Frie - de Got - tes, jen - seits all - en Ver -
The peace of God, which pass - eth all un - der -
T.
B.
p dolce
A
p
19
mp
- ste - hens,
-stand - ing,
wah - re eu - er Herz,
keep your hearts and minds,
mp
mp

23
cresc.
mf
wah - re eu - ren Sinn in dem Wis - sen um Got - tes
keep your hearts and minds in the know - ledge and love of
cresc.
mf
cresc.
mf
Sohns Je - sus Chris - tus, des
Son Je - sus Christ our
26
f dolce
Lieb' und der des Sohns Je - sus Chris - tus, des
God, and of his Son Je - sus Christ our
Sohns Je - sus Chris - tus, des
Son Je - sus Christ our
f dolce
f
30
mf
B
Herrn.
Lord:
mp dolce cantabile
unis.
mf
Und der Se - gen Got - tes des All -
and the bless - ing of God Al -
B
mf
mp

34
-mächt- 'gen, des Va - ters, des Sohns, und des
- migh - ty, the Fa - ther, the Son, and the
38
S.
A.
p
cresc.
mp
sei mit euch nun, sei mit
be a - mongst you, be a -
T.
B.
Heil - 'gen Geists,
Ho - ly Ghost,
p
cresc.
mp
p
cresc.
mp
42
cresc.
mf
cresc.
euch nun, sei mit euch von nun an und auf
- mongst you, be a - mongst you and re - main with you
euch nun,
-mongst you,
cresc.
mf
cresc.
cresc.
mf
cresc.

46
C
f
mp dolce e legato
e - wig. A - - - - men,
al - ways.
mp
dolce e legato
e - - wig. A - - - -
al - - ways.
mp dolce e legato
e - - wig. A -
al - - ways.
e - - wig. A - - - - - -
al - ways.
C
51
poco rit.
p
a - - men, a - - men,
- men, a - - - - men,
- - men, a - - men,
-men, a - - - - men, a - - men,
poco rit.

56 D a tempo
mp cresc.
a - -
mp cresc.
a - -
p cresc.
mp cresc.
a - - men, a - -
cresc.
mp cresc.
a - - men, a - - men, a - -
D a tempo
cresc.
mp cresc.
61
mf
mp
dim.
rall.
pp
-men, a - - men, a - men, a - men, a - men.
mf
mp
dim.
pp
-men, a - - - men, a - men, a - men.
mf
mp dim.
pp
-men, a - - - men, a - men, a - men.
mf
mp dim.
pp
-men, a - - men, a - - - - men.
rall.
mf
mp dim.
pp

*für das Clare College, Cambridge*

# Eine englische Segnung

## (A Clare Benediction)

Dt. Übers.: Moritz von Freyhold

Text und Musik
**JOHN RUTTER**

© Oxford University Press 1998 und 2023. Das Fotokopieren von Musiknoten ist GESETZLICH VERBOTEN.

16
SOPRAN und ALT
p
unis. mp
dich; und sein Geist weicht von dei-ner Sei - te nicht. In der
you; may his spi - rit be ev - er by your side. When you
Sw.
Ch.
21
A
cresc.
Nacht soll'n dich En - gel be - hü - ten; und am
sleep, may his an - gels watch o - ver you; when you
Sw.
cresc.
25
mf
SOPRAN und TENOR
cresc.
Tag zeigt er sei - ne Gna - de dir: Sollst ihn
wake, may he fill you with his grace: May you
mf
29
f ma dolce
dim.
SOPRAN und ALT
mp
lie - ben, ihm nah sein e - wig - lich und im
love him and serve him all your days, Then in
f ma dolce
dim.

33
(S. und A.)
unis.
Him - mel seh'n sein An - - ge - sicht.
hea - ven may you see his face.
Ch.
mp
38
B
p dolce
Mö - ge Gott sich dei - ner er-
May the Lord show his mer - cy up-
p dolce
B
Sw.
p
43
mp
-bar - men; sei - ne Wahr - heit ge - lei - te dich im Licht:
-on you; may the light of his pres-ence be your guide:
mp
poco cresc.
mp

48
Er schüt - ze und be-wahr' dich; und sein
May he guard you and up-hold you; may his
Ch.
53
Geist weicht von dei-ner Sei - te nicht.
spi - rit be ev-er by your side.
(mp)
In der
When you
Sw.

57
C
p
Ah
ah
cresc.
Nacht soll'n dich En - gel be - hü - ten;
sleep, may his an - gels watch o - ver you;
und am
when you
C
cresc.
61
cresc.
mf
Sollst ihn
May you
mf
Tag zeigt er sei - ne Gna - de dir:
wake, may he fill you with his grace:
Ch. oder Sw.
mf

poco rall.
a tempo
65
cresc.
f
dim.
und im
Then in
mp
lie - ben, ihm nah sein e - wig - lich
love him and serve him all your days,
cresc.
f
dim.
poco rall.
a tempo
cresc.
f
dim.
Him - mel seh'n sein An - - ge - sicht,
hea - ven may you see his face,
69
mp
A.
T.
B.
Summen
mp
Sw.
p
Man.
Ped.

74
seh'n sein An - -
may you see
dim.
und im Him - mel
Then in hea - ven
seh'n sein
may you
dim.
seh'n sein An - -
may you see
dim.
rall.
poco meno mosso
rit.
- ge - sicht,
his face,
78
p
dim.
pp
An - ge - sicht, seh'n sein An - ge - sicht.
see his face, may you see his face.
p
dim.
pp
-ge - sicht, An - ge - sicht.
his face, see his face.
rall.
poco meno mosso
rit.
Ch.
p
dim.
pp

# Für die Schönheit in der Welt

(For the beauty of the earth)

F. S. Pierpoint (1835–1917)
Dt. Übers.: Moritz von Freyhold

JOHN RUTTER

© Oxford University Press 1980 und 2023. Das Fotokopieren von Musiknoten ist GESETZLICH VERBOTEN.

17
Lieb', die mit viel Sinn
love which from our birth
20
Um uns war von An - be - ginn, um uns war von
O - ver and a - round us lies, o - ver and a -
23
mf
An - be - ginn: Herr, für dich wir stim - men
-round us lies: Lord of all, to thee we
mf
27
mp
an Un-sern fro - hen Lob - - ge -
raise This our joy - ful hymn of
mp

31
-sang.
praise.
35
A
SOPRAN
mf
ALT
2. Für den Tag und für die Nacht,
2. For the beau - ty of each hour
TENOR
BASS
mf
A
mf
39
All die schö - ne Zeit ver - bracht,
Of the day and of the night,
Baum und
Hill and

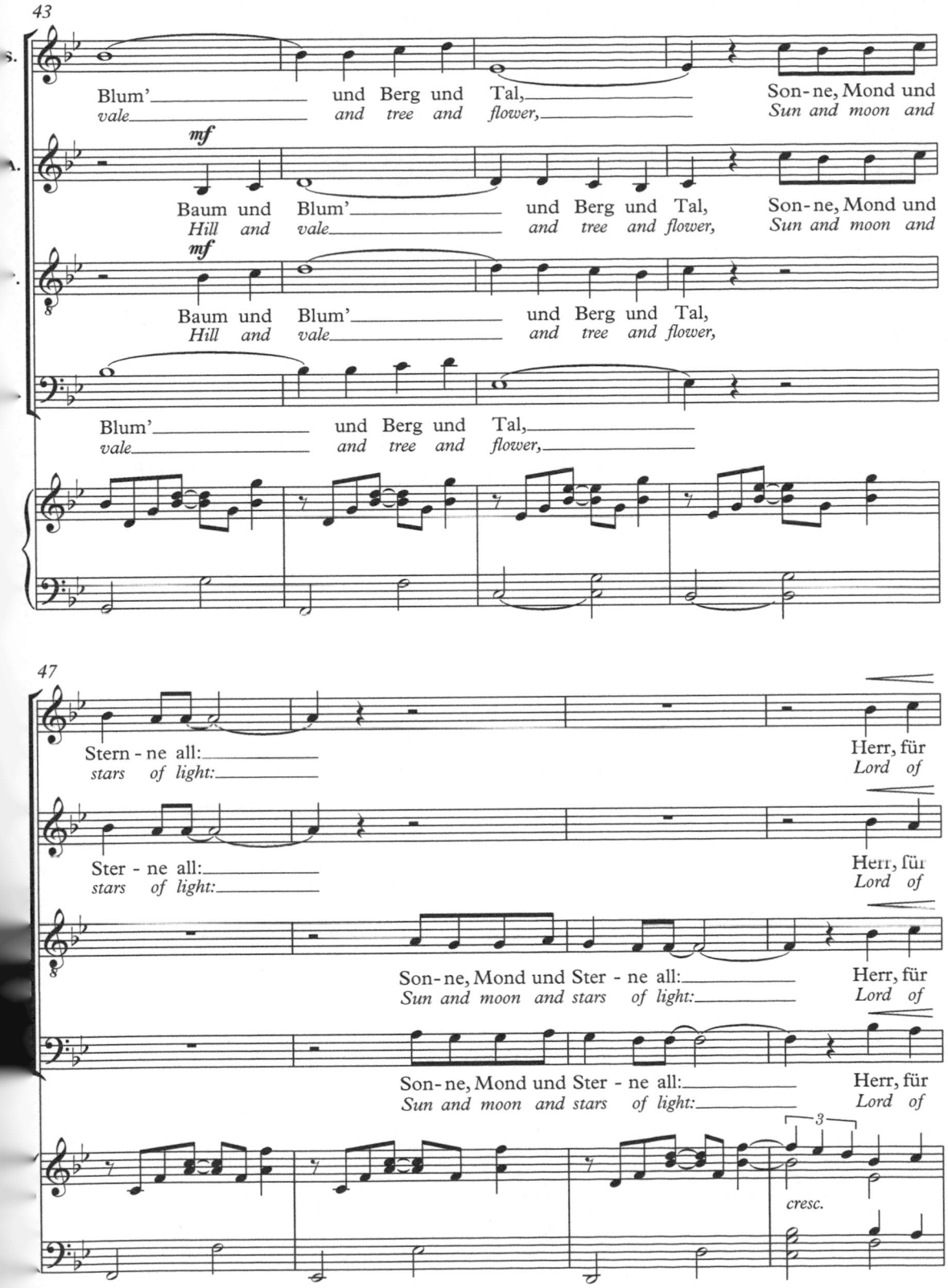
43
Blum' und Berg und Tal, Son-ne, Mond und
vale and tree and flower, Sun and moon and
mf
Baum und Blum' und Berg und Tal, Son-ne, Mond und
Hill and vale and tree and flower, Sun and moon and
mf
Baum und Blum' und Berg und Tal,
Hill and vale and tree and flower,
Blum' und Berg und Tal,
vale and tree and flower,
47
Stern-ne all: Herr, für
stars of light: Lord of
Ster-ne all: Herr, für
stars of light: Lord of
Son-ne, Mond und Ster-ne all: Herr, für
Sun and moon and stars of light: Lord of
Son-ne, Mond und Ster-ne all: Herr, für
Sun and moon and stars of light: Lord of
3
cresc.

51
f
dich wir stim - men an
all, to thee we raise
3
55
mf
Un - sern fro - hen Lob - - ge - sang.
This our joy - ful hymn of praise.
Un - - - sern Lob - ge - sang.
This our hymn of praise.
mp
Ped.

59
B
S.
A.
T.
B.
(T. und B.)
unis.
mp espress.
3. Für der Lie - be Se - lig -
3. For the joy of hu - man
B
p dolce
63
(S. und A.)
unis.
p
Für der Lie - be Se-lig-keit,
For the joy of love,
- keit,
love,
Bru - der, Schwes - ter, El - tern,
Bro - ther, sis - ter, pa - rent,
67
Bru-der, Schwes-ter, El - tern, Kind, Freun - de heut
Bro-ther, sis - ter, pa - rent, child, Friends on earth,
Kind,
child,
Freun - de heut und al - le
Friends on earth, and friends a -

71
(p)
und al - le Zeit,
and friends a - bove,
Für Ge -
For all
Zeit,
- bove,
Für Ge-dan-ken sanft und lind,
For all gen - tle thoughts and mild,
74
mf
- dan - ken
gen - tle
sanft und lind:
thoughts and mild:
Herr, für
Lord of
mf
für Ge-dan-ken sanft und lind:
for all gen - tle thoughts and mild:
Herr, für dich wir
Lord of all, to
mf
78
dich wir stim - men an
all, to thee we raise
mp
stim - men an
thee we raise
Un-sern fro - hen Lob-
This our joy - ful hymn
mp

82
unis. p
fro - hen Lob - ge - sang.
Our joy-ful hymn of praise.
- - - ge - sang.
of praise.
cresc.
85
C
SOPRAN
f
4. Schön - ste Ga - ben, die von dir
4. For each per - fect gift of thine
ALT, TENOR, BASS
unis. f
4. Schön - ste Ga - ben, die von dir
4. For each per - fect gift of thine
C
f
89
Uns ge - ge - ben wer - den hier,
To our race so free - ly giv - en,
mf
Uns ge - ge - ben wer - den hier,
To our race so free - ly giv - en,
Zier - en
Gra - ces
mf

93
mf
Zier - ren Mensch, Mensch und Gott - heit gleich,
Gra - ces hu - man and di - vine,
Mensch und Gott - heit gleich,
hu - man and di - vine,
96
Ah
Er - den-pracht und Him - mel - reich, Er-den-pracht und
Flow'rs of earth and buds of heav'n, flow'rs of earth and
99
S. f
A.
Ah Herr, für dich wir
Lord of all, to
cresc.
T.
B. f
Him - mel - reich:
buds of heav'n:
cresc.
f

102
S.
stim - men an
thee we raise
A.
stim - men an
thee we raise
T.
stim - men an
thee we raise
B.
stim - men an
thee we raise
105
D (♪ = ♪)
mf
Un - sern fro - hen Lob - - - ge - sang,
This our joy - ful hymn of praise,
Un - - - sern fro - hen Lob - ge - sang,
This our joy - ful hymn of praise,
Un - sern fro - hen Lob - - - ge - sang,
This our joy - ful hymn of praise,
Un - - - sern fro - hen Lob - ge - sang,
This our joy - ful hymn of praise,
D (♪ = ♪)
mf

111
rall.
(rallentando al fine)
p
Un - sern fro - hen Lob - - - ge -
This our joy - ful hymn of
Lob - ge -
our hymn of
Lob - ge -
our hymn of
Lob - ge -
our hymn of
rall.
(rallentando al fine)
dim.
p
114
molto rall.
- sang.
praise.
- sang.
praise.
- sang.
praise.
- sang.
praise.
molto rall.
p

*in memoriam Edward T. Chapman*

# Gott segne und behüt dich

(The Lord bless you and keep you)

Dt. Übers.: Alex Grendelmeier

**JOHN RUTTER**

© Oxford University Press 1981 und 1997. Das Fotokopieren von Musiknoten ist GESETZLICH VERBOTEN.

10
S.
A.
T.
B.
p dolce sempre
dir. Gott seg - ne und be - hüt dich, der
you. The Lord bless you and keep you: The
Gott seg - ne und be - hüt dich, der
The Lord bless you and keep you: The
13
mp
Herr las - se sein Ge - sicht er - strah - len, Ge - sicht er - strah - len und sei
Lord make his face to shine up - on you, to shine up - on you and be

16
(mp)
gnä - dig, und sei gnä - dig ü - ber dir. Gott
gra - cious, and be gra - cious un - to you: The
(mp)
gnä - dig, und sei gnä - dig ü - ber dir. Gott
gra - cious, and be gra - cious un - to you: The
gnä - dig, und sei gnä - dig ü - ber dir.
gra - cious, and be gra - cious un - to you:
gnä - dig, und sei gnä - dig ü - ber dir.
gra - cious, and be gra - cious un - to you.
19
cresc.
mf
wen - de dir das Licht sei - nes An - ge - sichts huld -
Lord lift up the light of his coun - te - nance up -
cresc.
mf
wen - de dir das Licht sei - nes An - ge - sichts huld -
Lord lift up the light of his coun - te - nance up -
cresc.
mf

22
- voll zu,
- on you,
- voll zu,
- on you,
mp cresc.
mf
Gott wen - de dir das Licht sei-nes
The Lord lift up the light of his
mp cresc.
mf
Gott wen - de dir das Licht sei-nes
The Lord lift up the light of his
cresc.
mf
25
mp
und schenk dir
and give you
An - ge-sichts huld - voll zu
coun - te-nance up - on you
An - ge-sichts huld - voll zu
coun - te-nance up - on you
dim.
mp

28
dim.
Frie - den,
peace,
p
dim.
und schenk dir Frie - den,
and give you peace,
dim.
p
dim.
31
pp
p
und schenk dir Frie - den, und schenk dir
and give you peace, and give you
pp
p
und schenk dir Frie - den, und schenk dir
and give you peace, and give you
pp
p
und schenk dir Frie - den, und schenk dir
and give you peace, and give you
pp
p
und schenk dir Frie - den, und schenk dir
and give you peace, and give you
pp

34
poco rit.
a tempo
Frie - - den.
peace.
Frie - - den.
peace.
mp
Frie - den. A - - - - - men,
peace.
mp
Frie - den. A - - - - - men,
peace.
poco rit.
a tempo
(Ch. oder Gt.)
cresc.
mp
37
mf
f
a - - - - men, a - - -
mf
f
a - - men, a - - men, a - men,
mf
f
a - - - - men,
cresc.
mf
f
a - men, a - men, a - - -
cresc.
mf cresc.
f

40
mf
mp
men, a - men, a - - men,
mf
mp
a - men, a - - men, a - -
mf
mp
a - - men, a - - - men, a - -
mf
mp
men, a - men,
mf dim.
p
43
rall.
molto rall.
p dim.
pp
a - men, a - - - - men.
p dim.
pp
men, a - - - men.
p dim.
pp
men, a - - - - men.
p dim.
pp
a - - - - - - - men.
rall.
Sw.
molto rall.
dim.
pp

# Gott sei stets in mir

## (God be in my head)

Worte aus dem Gebetbuch Sarum Primer (1514)

Dt. Übers.: Moritz von Freyhold

**JOHN RUTTER**

© Oxford University Press Inc. 1970. Assigned to Oxford University Press 2010. This edition © Oxford University Press 2023.
Das Fotokopieren von Musiknoten ist GESETZLICH VERBOTEN.

9
p
mei - nem Schau - en. Gott im Mun - de sei
look - - - - ing. God be in my mouth
mei - nem Schau - en. Gott im Mun - de sei
look - - - - ing. God be in my mouth
mei - nem Schau - en. Gott im Mun - de sei
look - - - - ing. God be in my mouth
mei - nem Schau - en. Gott im Mun - de sei
look - - - - ing. God be in my mouth
13
mf
p
und in mei - nen Wor - ten. Gott im
and in my speak - - - ing. God be
und in mei - nen Wor - ten. Gott im
and in my speak - - - ing. God be
und in mei - nen Wor - ten. Gott im
and in my speak - - - ing. God be
und in mei - nen Wor - ten. Gott im
and in my speak - - - ing. God be

17
Poco meno mosso
pp
Her - zen sei, in mei - nem Den - ken. Gott sei
in mine heart and in my think - ing. God be
Her - zen sei, in mei - nem Den - ken. Gott sei
in mine heart and in my think - ing. God be
Her - zen sei, in mei - nem Den - ken. Gott sei
in mine heart and in my think - ing. God be
Her - zen sei, in mei - nem Den - ken. Gott sei
in mine heart and in my think - ing. God be
Poco meno mosso
pp
21
rit.
pp
ppp
da am End', wenn ich muss Ab - schied neh - - men.
at my end and in my de - part - - ing.
da am End', wenn ich muss Ab - schied neh - men.
at my end and in my de - part - ing.
da am End', wenn ich muss Ab - schied neh - men.
at my end and in my de - part - ing.
da am End', wenn ich muss Ab - schied neh - - men.
at my end and in my de - part - - ing.
rit.
pp
ppp

*Vom Chorleiterverband Texas beauftragt*

# Öffne mir die Augen

## (Open thou mine eyes)

Lancelot Andrewes (1555–1626)
Dt. Übers.: Moritz von Freyhold

**JOHN RUTTER**

**Fließend und nachdenklich; ziemlich „frei"** ♩ = *c.*63

**SOLO SOPRAN (oder kleiner Chor)**

*mp legato*

Öff-ne mir die Au - gen, dass ich seh', Reg an mein Herz, dass ich be-
*O-pen thou mine eyes and I shall see: In-cline my heart and I shall de-*

5 *cresc.* *mf* > *mp* *dim.* *p*

-geh-re: Lenk mei-ne Schrit-te, so dass ich lauf' Auf dem Weg der Ge - bo - te.
*-sire: Or - der my steps and I shall walk In the ways of thy com-mand-ments.*

10 **SOPRAN (alle)** *mp*

S. Öff-ne mir die Au - gen, dass ich seh', Reg an mein Herz, dass ich be-
*O-pen thou mine eyes and I shall see: In-cline my heart and I shall de-*

**ALT** *mp*

A. Öff-ne mir die Au-gen, dass ich seh', Reg an mein Herz, dass ich be-
*O-pen thou mine eyes and I shall see: In-cline my heart and I shall de-*

*nur zum Proben* *mp*

14 *cresc.* *mf* > *mp* *dim.*

- geh - re: Lenk mei-ne Schrit-te, so dass ich lauf' Auf dem Weg der Ge-
*- sire: Or - der my steps and I shall walk In the ways of thy com-*

*cresc.* *mf* > *mp* *dim.*

- geh - re: Lenk mei-ne Schrit - te, so dass ich lauf' Auf dem Weg der Ge-
*- sire: Or - der my steps and I shall walk In the ways of thy com-*

*cresc.* *mf* > *mp* *dim.*

© Oxford University Press Inc., 1980. Assigned to Oxford University Press 2010. This edition © Oxford University Press 2023.
Das Fotokopieren von Musiknoten ist GESETZLICH VERBOTEN.

18
S.
p
- bo - te.
- mand - ments.
A.
p
- bo - te.
- mand - ments.
T.
mp dolce
cresc.
Oh Herr, oh sei ein Gott für mich, Lass kein'
O Lord God, be thou to me a God And be -
B.
mp dolce
cresc.
Oh Herr, oh sei ein Gott für mich, Lass kein'
O Lord God, be thou to me a God And be -
mp dolce
cresc.
21
mf
mp
An - de - ren ne - ben dir sein, Kein' An - de - ren ne - ben dir
- side thee let there be none else, No oth - er, naught else with
mf
mp
An - de - ren ne - ben dir sein, Kein' An - de - ren ne - ben dir
- side thee let there be none else, No oth - er, naught else with
mf
mp

24
p legato
cresc.
Lass mich Dich eh-ren im-mer-zu und dir die-nen Und fol-gen
Vouch-safe to me to wor-ship thee and serve thee Ac-cord-ing
Lass mich Dich eh-ren im-mer-zu, dir die - nen Und fol-gen
Vouch-safe to me to wor-ship thee and serve thee Ac-cord-ing
p
sein, Dich eh-ren und dir die - nen Und fol-gen
thee, to wor-ship thee and serve thee Ac-cord-ing
sein, Dich eh-ren und dir die - nen Und fol-gen
thee, to wor ship thee and serve thee Ac-cord-ing
27
mp cresc.
dei - nen Ge-bo-ten, Im wah-ren Gei-ste, mit mei - nem
to thy com-mand-ments, In truth of spi-rit, In rev-'rence of
dei - nen Ge-bo-ten, Im wah-ren Gei-ste, mit mei - nem
to thy com-mand-ments, In truth of spi-rit, In rev-'rence of
dei - nen Ge-bo-ten, Im wah-ren Gei-ste, mit mei - nem
to thy com-mand-ments, In truth of spi-rit, In rev-'rence of
dei - nen Ge-bo-ten, Im wah-ren Gei-ste, mit mei - nem
to thy com-mand-ments, In truth of spi-rit, In rev-'rence of

30
mf
dim.
mp
Lei - be, Mit mei - nem Wort, Al - lein und mit an - dern.
bo - dy, In bless - ing of lips, In pri - vate and in pub - lic.
Lei - be, Mit mei - nem Wort, Al - lein und mit an - dern.
bo - dy, In bless - ing of lips, In pri - vate and pub - lic.
Lei - be, Mit mei - nem Wort, Al - lein und mit an - dern.
bo - dy, In bless - ing of lips, In pri - vate and pub - lic.
Lei - be, Mit mei - nem Wort, Al - lein und mit an - dern.
bo - dy, In bless - ing of lips, In pri - vate and pub - lic.
33
SOLO SOPRAN (oder kleiner Chor)
mp
Öff - ne mir die Au - gen, dass ich seh': Reg an mein Herz, dass ich be-
O - pen thou mine eyes and I shall see: In - cline my heart and I shall de-
p
Summen
Summen
Summen
Summen

37
cresc.
mf
dim.
-geh - re: Lenk mei - ne Schrit - te, so dass ich lauf' Auf dem
- sire: Or - der my steps and I shall walk In the
unis.
40
(dim.)
rit.
p
Weg der Ge - bo - te.
ways of thy com - mand - ments.

*zur Feier des 70. Jubiläums des Council for the Protection of Rural England*

# Schau auf die Welt

(Look at the world)

Dt. Übers.: Hermann Eckel

Text und Musik
**JOHN RUTTER**

© Oxford University Press 1996 und 2023. Das Fotokopieren von Musiknoten ist GESETZTLICH VERBOTEN.

17
Schau auf die Welt: so vie-le schö-ne Din-ge,
Look at the world: so ma-ny joys and won-ders,
21
so vie-le Wun-der auf un-serm Weg.
So ma-ny mi-ra-cles a-long our way.
A
S. (und KINDER)
25
mf
A.
Lob sei dir, o Herr, für dei-ne Schöp-fung,
Praise to thee, O Lord, for all cre-a-tion,
T.
mf
B.
A
mf
(Ped.)

29
Lass uns dank - bar sein, auf daß wir sehn:
Give us thank - ful hearts, that we may see:
33
dim.
Al - le gu - ten Ga - ben, al - ler Se - gen,
All the gifts we share, and ev - 'ry bless - ing,
dim.
dim.
37
mp
all dies kommt von dir.
All things come of thee.
mp
mp
cresc.

41
B
KINDER (oder SOPRAN und ALT)
unis. mf
2. Schau auf die Erd,
2. Look at the earth
mf
45
die uns be - schenkt mit Blu - men;
bring - ing forth fruit and flow - er;
Schau auf den Him - mel, die
Look at the sky, the
49
TENOR und BASS
unis. mf
Son - ne und den Re - gen;
sun - shine and the rain;
Schau auf die Hü - gel,
Look at the hills,
53
SOPRAN und ALT
unis. mf
schau auch auf Wald und Ber - ge,
look at the trees and moun - tains,
Tä - ler und
Val - ley and

56
kla - re Was - ser, Feld und Flur:
flow - ing ri - ver, field and plain:
59
C
f
S.
A.
Lob sei dir, o Herr, für dei - ne Schöp - fung,
Praise to thee, O Lord, for all cre - a - tion,
T.
B.
f
C
f
63
Lass uns dank - bar sein, auf daß wir sehn:
Give us thank - ful hearts, that we may see:

67
mf
dim.
Al - - le gu - ten Ga - ben, al - ler Se - gen,
All the gifts we share, and ev - 'ry bless - ing,
mf
dim.
mf
dim.
71
mp
all dies kommt von dir.
All things come of thee.
mp
mp
mf
75
D
KINDER (oder TENOR und BASS)
unis. mp legato
3. Denk an den Früh - ling,
3. Think of the spring,
mp legato

79
denk an den war - men Som - mer. Bring ein die Ern - te, be -
think of the warmth of sum - mer Bring - ing the har - vest be -
83
- vor der Win - ter kommt. Al - les ge -
- fore the win - ter's cold. Ev - 'ry - thing
86
- deiht, al - les hat sei - ne Zeit,
grows, ev - 'ry - thing has a sea - son,
89
Al - les wird ein - ge - bracht zu Got - tes Ehr:
Till it is ga - thered to the Fa - ther's fold:

* Begleitung nur für die Unisono-Aufführung.

108
F
ALLE STIMMEN
unis. f
4. Sämt - li - che
4. Ev - 'ry good
(cresc.)
f
112
Ga - ben, die wir ver - ehr'n und prei - sen,
gift, all that we need and che - rish
115
kom - men von Gott als Zei - chen sei - ner Lieb;
Comes from the Lord in to - ken of his love;
119
(TENOR und BASS)
mf
Wir sind sein Werk, We - sen von Got - tes Gna - den;
We are his hands, stew - ards of all his boun - ty;
mf

123
(SOPRAN und ALT)
unis. mf
cresc.
sein ist die Erd, und sein das Him - mel - reich:
His is the earth, and his the heav'ns a - bove:
cresc.
127
G
f
S.
A.
Lob sei dir, o Herr, für dei - ne Schöp - fung,
Praise to thee, O Lord, for all cre - a - tion,
T.
B.
f
G
f
131
dim.
lass uns dank - bar sein, auf daß wir sehn:
Give us thank - ful hearts, that we may see:
dim.
dim.

135
mf
dim.
Al - - le gu - ten Ga - ben, al - ler Se - gen,
All the gifts we share, and ev - 'ry bless - ing,
mf
dim.
mf
dim.
139
mp
all dies kommt von dir,
All things come of thee,
mp
mp
dim.
143
rall. al fine
p
all dies kommt von dir.
all things come of thee.
p
rall. al fine
p